THE ULTIMATE GUIDE TO MAKING PASSIVE INCOME

Genevieve Velzian

Copyright © 2024 Genevieve Velzian

All rights reserved

All recommendations made in this book are the author's own and in no way replace legal or healthcare advice. Please seek your own legal counsel. The author accepts no liability.

No part of this book may be reproduced, or stored in a retrieval system, or transmitted in any form or by any means, electronic, mechanical, photocopying, recording, or otherwise, without express written permission of the publisher.

INTRODUCTION TO PASSIVE INCOME

In the realm of personal finance, the concept of passive income is often celebrated as the key to financial freedom. Unlike active income, which requires continuous effort and time, passive income allows you to earn money with minimal ongoing work. This chapter aims to provide a detailed understanding of what passive income is, how it differs from other forms of income, and why it is an essential component of a robust financial strategy.

What is Passive Income?

Passive income is money earned with little to no daily effort once the initial setup is complete. It flows in regularly, providing financial stability and freedom. Common examples include rental income, dividends from stocks, royalties from creative work, and earnings from an online business.

Different Types of Income

To fully grasp the significance of passive income, it's helpful to differentiate it from other types of income:

Active Income: This is the most familiar form of income for most people. It includes wages, salaries, tips, and any other earnings where you exchange time for money. If you stop working, the income stops as well.

Portfolio Income: Derived from investments such as stocks, bonds, and mutual funds. While it can require active management, it often involves earning money through capital gains, interest, and dividends.

Passive Income: As mentioned, this income requires minimal effort to maintain. It's not tied to the amount of time you spend working, making it a powerful tool for financial independence.

Characteristics of Passive Income Streams

Not all passive income streams are created equal. Some key characteristics to consider include:

Initial Effort: Most passive income sources require significant upfront effort or investment. This could be in the form of time, money, or both.

Scalability: A good passive income stream should have the potential to grow without a proportional increase in effort. For example, selling a digital product can generate more income as more units are sold, without additional work per unit.

Sustainability: The best passive income sources continue to generate revenue with little ongoing maintenance. For instance, rental properties need occasional upkeep, but they provide a steady income stream.

How Passive Income Can Transform Financial Stability

Building passive income streams can drastically alter your financial landscape. Here's how:

Financial Freedom: With passive income, you're not tied to a 9-to-5 job. This freedom allows you to spend your time as you wish, pursue passions, travel, or even retire early.

Income Diversification: Relying solely on active income can be risky. If you lose your job or are unable to work, your income stops. Passive income provides a safety net, ensuring that you have multiple revenue streams.

Wealth Building: Passive income allows your money to work for you. Reinvesting earnings from passive income sources can compound your wealth over time, leading to greater financial security.

Common Misconceptions

There are several misconceptions about passive income that can lead to unrealistic expectations:

It's Effortless: While the goal is to earn money with minimal effort, the initial setup often requires significant work and dedication.

Instant Wealth: Building substantial passive income takes time. It's not a get-rich-quick scheme but rather a long-term strategy.

Risk-Free: Like any investment, passive income streams come with risks. It's essential to do thorough research and due diligence to mitigate these risks.

Overview of the Book's Structure

This book is designed to guide you through various strategies for generating passive income. Each chapter will delve into a specific method, providing practical advice, real-life examples, and actionable steps to get you started. From real estate investments to digital products and online businesses, you will find a wealth of information to help you build a diversified portfolio of passive income streams.

In the next chapter, we will explore how to set the foundation for creating passive income, including assessing your current financial situation, setting goals, and developing the right mindset. By laying a strong groundwork, you will be better prepared to embark on your journey towards financial freedom.

SETTING THE FOUNDATION

Introduction

Before diving into the various methods of generating passive income, it is crucial to lay a solid foundation. This involves assessing your current financial situation, setting clear and achievable goals, developing the right mindset, and building the initial capital required. This chapter will guide you through these essential steps, ensuring that you are well-prepared for the journey ahead.

Assessing Your Current Financial Situation

The first step in setting the foundation is to gain a clear understanding of your current financial situation. This involves a comprehensive evaluation of your income, expenses, assets, and liabilities. Here's how to go about it:

Income and Expenses: Track all sources of income and itemise your monthly expenses. This will help you identify areas where you can cut costs and save more money for investing in passive income streams.

Assets and Liabilities: Make a list of all your assets (e.g., savings, investments, property) and liabilities (e.g., loans, credit card debt). Understanding your net worth will give you a clear picture of your financial health.

Cash Flow Analysis: Analyse your cash flow to ensure that you have a positive net cash flow each month. This means that your income exceeds your expenses, providing surplus funds for investment.

Setting Financial Goals

Once you have a clear understanding of your financial situation, the next step is to set financial goals. These goals will provide direction and motivation as you work towards building passive income. Consider the following:

Short-term Goals: These are objectives you aim to achieve within the next year. Examples include paying off high-interest debt, building an emergency fund, or saving a specific amount for investment.

Medium-term Goals: These goals typically span one to five years. They might include saving for a home deposit, increasing your investment portfolio, or achieving a certain level of passive income.

Long-term Goals: Long-term goals are those you plan to achieve over a period of five years or more. Examples include financial independence, early retirement, or generating enough passive income to cover all living expenses.

Developing the Right Mindset

Building passive income streams requires a strong and resilient mindset. It's not a path to instant wealth but rather a long-term strategy that demands patience, discipline, and perseverance. Here are some key mindset principles to adopt:

Growth Mindset: Embrace the belief that you can learn and grow in your financial knowledge and skills. View challenges as opportunities to learn rather than obstacles.

Patience and Persistence: Understand that building passive income takes time and effort. Stay committed to your goals, even when progress seems slow.

Risk Tolerance: Be prepared to take calculated risks. Passive income opportunities often involve some level of risk, and being comfortable with this is essential.

Continuous Learning: Stay informed and continually educate yourself about different passive income strategies. The financial landscape is always evolving, and staying updated will help you make informed decisions.

Building Initial Capital

Most passive income streams require an initial investment, whether it be money, time, or both. Here are some strategies to build the capital needed to start your passive income journey:

Save Aggressively: Identify and eliminate unnecessary expenses. Redirect these savings towards your investment fund.

Increase Income: Look for ways to increase your income, such as taking on a part-time job, freelancing, or starting a side business. Use this extra income to fund your passive income ventures.

Leverage Existing Assets: Utilise any existing assets you have. For instance, if you own property, consider renting out a room or using it as collateral for a loan to invest in other opportunities.

Smart Debt Management: If you have high-interest debt, prioritise paying it off. Once cleared, you can reallocate the funds used for debt payments towards investments.

Conclusion

Setting a strong foundation is crucial for success in building passive income streams. By assessing your financial situation, setting clear goals, developing the right mindset, and building initial capital, you are well-prepared to embark on this journey. In the next chapter, we will delve into one of the most popular and lucrative forms of passive income: real estate investments. This will provide you with a practical and comprehensive guide to generating income through property.

REAL ESTATE INTRODUCTION

Real estate has long been considered one of the most reliable and lucrative forms of passive income. By investing in property, you can generate a steady stream of rental income, benefit from property appreciation, and take advantage of various tax benefits. This chapter will explore different real estate investment strategies, providing practical advice on how to get started and maximise your returns.

Types of Real Estate Investments

There are several ways to invest in real estate, each with its own set of benefits and challenges. Here are some of the most common methods:

Rental Properties: Purchasing residential or commercial properties to rent out to tenants is one of the most direct ways to earn passive income from real estate. This method requires hands-on management or hiring a property manager.

Real Estate Investment Trusts (REITs): REITs allow you to invest in a portfolio of properties without owning them directly. They are traded on major stock exchanges, providing liquidity and diversification.

Real Estate Crowdfunding: This involves pooling funds with other investors to invest in larger real estate projects. Crowdfunding platforms offer access to both residential and commercial properties.

Vacation Rentals and Airbnb: Short-term rentals can be more profitable than long-term leases, especially in popular tourist destinations. Platforms like Airbnb make it easier to manage bookings and communicate with guests.

Steps to Getting Started with Real Estate Investments

Investing in real estate requires careful planning and research. Here are the steps to help you get started:

Research the Market: Understand the local real estate market where you plan to invest. Look at property prices, rental yields, occupancy rates, and future growth prospects. Research different neighbourhoods to find areas with high demand and potential for appreciation.

Set a Budget: Determine how much you can afford to invest. Consider the costs of purchasing the property, ongoing maintenance, property management fees, and potential vacancies. Ensure you have a financial buffer for unexpected expenses.

Choose the Right Property: Look for properties that align with your investment goals. For rental properties, consider the type of tenants you want to attract and the amenities they would value. For vacation rentals, focus on properties in desirable locations with high tourist traffic.

Finance Your Investment: Explore different financing options, such as mortgages, home equity loans, or partnerships with other investors. Compare interest rates, loan terms, and down payment requirements to find the best deal.

Conduct Due Diligence: Before purchasing a property, perform a thorough inspection to identify any issues that could affect its value or rental potential. Review the property's history, including previous ownership, maintenance records, and any legal encumbrances.

Managing Rental Properties

Effective property management is crucial for maximising your rental income and ensuring the long-term success of your investment. Here are some tips for managing rental properties:

Screen Tenants Carefully: Conduct background checks, credit checks, and reference checks to ensure you choose reliable tenants who will pay rent on time and take care of the property.

Set Competitive Rent Prices: Research local rental rates to set a competitive price that will attract tenants while maximising your income. Consider offering incentives for long-term leases to reduce turnover.

Maintain the Property: Regular maintenance and prompt repairs are essential to keep your property in good condition and retain its value. Address any issues reported by tenants promptly to maintain a positive relationship.

Hire a Property Manager: If you prefer a hands-off approach, consider hiring a property manager to handle tenant interactions, maintenance, and rent collection. This will reduce your workload but will incur additional costs.

Benefits of Real Estate Investments

Investing in real estate offers several advantages, making it an attractive option for generating passive income:

Steady Cash Flow: Rental properties provide a regular income stream, which can be particularly valuable during retirement or times of economic uncertainty.

Appreciation: Real estate tends to appreciate over time, allowing you to build wealth as property values increase. This can provide significant returns when you decide to sell the property.

Tax Benefits: Real estate investors can take advantage of various tax deductions, including mortgage interest, property taxes, depreciation, and maintenance expenses. These deductions can significantly reduce your taxable income.

Leverage: Real estate allows you to use leverage, meaning you can borrow money to purchase properties and amplify your returns. This can increase your purchasing power and potential profits.

Inflation Hedge: Real estate often performs well during inflationary periods, as property values and rental income tend to rise with inflation, preserving your purchasing power.

Challenges and Risks

While real estate can be highly profitable, it also comes with risks and challenges that you need to be aware of:

Market Fluctuations: Property values can fluctuate due to economic conditions, changes in interest rates, and local market dynamics. This can affect your rental income and the value of your investment.

Vacancies: Periods of vacancy can reduce your rental income and increase your costs. It's essential to have a financial cushion to cover these periods and maintain a high occupancy rate through effective marketing.

Maintenance Costs: Properties require ongoing maintenance and repairs, which can be costly. Unexpected issues, such as plumbing or electrical problems, can also arise, requiring immediate attention and funds.

Tenant Issues: Dealing with problematic tenants can be stressful and time-consuming. Non-payment of rent, property damage, and legal disputes are potential challenges you may encounter.

Conclusion

Real estate investments offer a powerful way to generate passive income and build long-term wealth. By understanding the different types of real estate investments, conducting thorough research, and managing properties effectively, you can maximise your returns and achieve financial independence.

In the next chapter, we will explore dividend investing, another popular and accessible method for generating passive income. This will provide you with insights on how to build a portfolio of dividend-paying stocks and create a reliable income stream.nvestments

DIVIDEND INVESTING

Introduction

Dividend investing is a popular and accessible method for generating passive income. By investing in dividend-paying stocks, you can earn regular income in the form of dividends, which are portions of a company's earnings distributed to shareholders. This chapter will explore the fundamentals of dividend investing, how to choose the right stocks, and strategies to build a robust dividend portfolio.

Understanding Dividends

Dividends are payments made by a corporation to its shareholders, usually as a distribution of profits. These payments can be made in cash, additional shares of stock, or other forms. Dividends provide a way for investors to share in the company's success and receive a return on their investment.

Types of Dividends:

Cash Dividends: The most common type, where investors receive cash payments.
Stock Dividends: Additional shares of stock given to shareholders.
Special Dividends: One-time payments made in addition to regular dividends, often due to extraordinary earnings or events.
Dividend Yield: This is a financial ratio that shows how much a company pays out in dividends each year relative to its stock price.

Benefits of Dividend Investing

Dividend investing offers several advantages, making it an attractive strategy for generating passive income:

Regular Income: Dividends provide a steady income stream, which can be particularly useful for retirees or those seeking financial independence.

Compounding Returns: Reinvesting dividends through dividend reinvestment plans (DRIPs) allows investors to buy more shares, leading to compound growth over time.

Stability and Reliability: Dividend-paying companies are often well-established and financially stable, making them less volatile than non-dividend-paying stocks.

Inflation Hedge: Dividends can provide a hedge against inflation, as companies often increase their dividend payments over time, maintaining the purchasing power of your income.

Choosing Dividend-Paying Stocks

Selecting the right dividend-paying stocks is crucial for building a successful dividend portfolio. Here are some key factors to consider:

Dividend History: Look for companies with a long track record of paying and increasing dividends. Consistent dividend growth is a positive indicator of financial health and management's commitment to returning value to shareholders.

Dividend Yield: Aim for stocks with a healthy dividend yield. However, be cautious of yields that are significantly higher than the market average, as they may indicate potential financial trouble or unsustainable payouts.

Payout Ratio: This ratio shows the proportion of earnings a company pays out as dividends. A lower payout ratio suggests that the company retains enough earnings to invest in growth and sustain future dividends. Ideally, look for companies with payout ratios below 60%.

Financial Health: Assess the company's financial health by reviewing its balance sheet, income statement, and cash flow statement. Strong cash flow and low debt levels are positive indicators.

Industry and Market Position: Consider companies in stable and growing industries. Companies with a dominant market position and competitive advantages are more likely to maintain and grow their dividends.

Building a Dividend Portfolio

A well-diversified dividend portfolio can provide reliable income and reduce risk. Here's how to build one:

Diversification: Spread your investments across various sectors and industries to reduce risk. Avoid concentrating too much in one sector, even if it offers high yields.

Dividend Growth Stocks: Include stocks with a history of dividend growth. These companies are likely to continue increasing their dividends, providing a growing income stream.

High-Yield Stocks: Balance your portfolio with some high-yield stocks for immediate income. Ensure these companies are financially stable to avoid the risk of dividend cuts.

Reinvest Dividends: Use DRIPs to reinvest your dividends and buy more shares. This can accelerate the growth of your portfolio through compounding.

Monitor and Rebalance: Regularly review your portfolio to ensure it aligns with your investment goals. Rebalance as necessary to maintain diversification and optimise returns.

Risks and Challenges

While dividend investing has many benefits, it also comes with risks and challenges:

Dividend Cuts: Companies may reduce or eliminate dividends during financial difficulties, affecting your income stream. Diversification can mitigate this risk.

Interest Rate Risk: Rising interest rates can make dividend-paying stocks less attractive compared to fixed-income investments like bonds, potentially leading to price declines.

Market Volatility: Dividend stocks are still subject to market fluctuations. While they may be less volatile than non-dividend stocks, they can still experience significant price changes.

Tax Considerations: Dividends are often subject to taxes, which can reduce your net returns. Be aware of the tax implications in your country and consider tax-advantaged accounts to minimise the impact.

Conclusion

Dividend investing is a powerful strategy for generating passive income and building long-term wealth. By understanding how dividends work, selecting quality dividend-paying stocks, and building a diversified portfolio, you can create a reliable income stream that supports your financial goals.

In the next chapter, we will explore online businesses, another exciting and potentially lucrative avenue for generating passive income. This will provide insights into various online business models and how to set up and manage them effectively.

ONLINE BUSINESSES

Introduction

In the digital age, online businesses offer a unique and scalable way to generate passive income. With the internet's global reach, you can create a business that operates 24/7 and reaches customers worldwide. This chapter will explore various online business models, providing practical advice on how to set them up, manage them efficiently, and scale them for maximum profitability.

Types of Online Businesses

There are numerous online business models to consider, each with its own set of benefits and challenges. Here are some of the most popular:

E-commerce Stores: Selling physical or digital products through an online store. Platforms like Shopify, WooCommerce, and BigCommerce make it easy to set up and manage an e-commerce site.

Dropshipping: A form of e-commerce where you sell products without holding inventory. When a customer places an order, the supplier ships the product directly to them. This reduces upfront costs and storage requirements.

Print-on-Demand: Selling custom-designed products like T-shirts, mugs, and phone cases. Services like Printful and Teespring handle production and shipping, allowing you to focus on design and marketing.

Affiliate Marketing: Promoting other companies' products and earning a commission for each sale made through your referral links. Affiliate marketing can be done through blogs, social media, or dedicated review sites.

Subscription Services: Offering products or services on a subscription basis. This model provides a steady and predictable income stream. Examples include subscription boxes, online courses, and software-as-a-service (SaaS).

Digital Products: Creating and selling digital products such as e-books, online courses, software, and templates. Digital products have high profit margins and can be sold repeatedly without additional production costs.

Setting Up an Online Business

Starting an online business requires careful planning and execution. Here are the steps to get started:

Identify a Niche: Choose a niche that you are passionate about and that has market demand. Conduct market research to understand your target audience, their needs, and preferences.

Create a Business Plan: Outline your business goals, target market, revenue model, and marketing strategy. A well-thought-out business plan will guide your efforts and help secure funding if needed.

Choose a Platform: Select an online platform that suits your business model. For e-commerce, consider platforms like Shopify or WooCommerce. For affiliate marketing, create a blog or website using WordPress.

Build Your Online Presence: Design a professional and user-friendly website. Ensure it is mobile-friendly, loads quickly, and provides a seamless user experience. Create valuable content to attract and engage your audience.

Set Up Payment and Shipping: Integrate payment gateways like PayPal, Stripe, or Square to accept payments. For physical products, set up shipping options and calculate costs.

Source Products: If you're selling physical products, find reliable suppliers or manufacturers. For digital products, create high-quality content or software that addresses your audience's needs.

Managing an Online Business

Effective management is crucial for the success of your online business. Here are some tips:

Automate Processes: Use automation tools to streamline repetitive tasks like email marketing, social media posting, and order processing. This will free up your time to focus on growth and strategy.

Monitor Performance: Use analytics tools to track website traffic, sales, and customer behaviour. Regularly review this data to identify trends and make informed decisions.

Customer Service: Provide excellent customer service to build trust and loyalty. Respond promptly to inquiries, handle complaints professionally, and seek feedback to improve your offerings.

Inventory Management: For e-commerce businesses, manage your inventory efficiently to avoid stockouts and overstocking. Use inventory management software to track stock levels and forecast demand.

Marketing: Implement a robust marketing strategy to drive traffic and sales. Use a mix of SEO, content marketing, social media, email marketing, and paid advertising to reach your target audience.

Scaling Your Online Business

Once your online business is up and running, you can focus on scaling it to increase profitability:

Expand Product Line: Introduce new products or services that complement your existing offerings. This can attract new customers and increase sales from existing ones.

Increase Traffic: Invest in marketing to drive more traffic to your website. Use SEO to improve organic search rankings, run paid ads, and leverage social media to reach a wider audience.

Optimise Conversion Rates: Improve your website's user experience to increase the percentage of visitors who make a purchase. A/B test different elements like headlines, images, and call-to-action buttons to see what works best.

Outsource and Delegate: As your business grows, consider outsourcing tasks like customer service, content creation, and order fulfilment. This allows you to focus on strategic growth.

Explore New Markets: Expand your business internationally by offering products in multiple languages and accepting different currencies. This can significantly increase your customer base.

Case Study: Successful Online Business

To illustrate the potential of online businesses, consider the case of John, who started an e-commerce store selling handmade jewellery. By following the steps outlined above, John identified a niche market, created a beautiful and functional website, and leveraged social media to drive traffic. He used automation tools to manage his inventory and customer orders efficiently. Over time, he expanded his product line, increased his marketing efforts, and saw significant growth. Today, John's business generates substantial passive income, allowing him to focus on new ventures and enjoy a flexible lifestyle.

Conclusion

Online businesses offer a scalable and flexible way to generate passive income. By choosing the right business model, setting up your business efficiently, and focusing on growth and automation, you can create a profitable online venture.

In the next chapter, we will delve into digital products, exploring how to create and sell them effectively to generate passive income. This will provide you with practical insights into tapping into the lucrative market of digital goods.

DIGITAL PRODUCTS

Introduction

Digital products have revolutionised the way people create and consume content. Unlike physical products, digital products can be produced once and sold repeatedly with minimal overhead costs. This scalability makes them an attractive option for generating passive income. In this chapter, we will explore various types of digital products, how to create and market them, and strategies for maximising their potential.

Types of Digital Products

Digital products come in various forms, each offering unique opportunities for passive income. Here are some of the most popular types:

E-books: E-books are digital versions of written content that can be read on e-readers, tablets, or computers. They cover a wide range of topics, from fiction to self-help and technical guides.

Online Courses: These are structured educational materials delivered over the internet. They can include video lectures, written content, quizzes, and interactive elements. Platforms like Udemy, Teachable, and Coursera make it easy to create and sell online courses.

Software and Apps: Developing software or mobile applications can be highly lucrative. Once developed, these products can be sold or offered on a subscription basis.

Printables and Templates: These include downloadable files such as planners, calendars, business templates, and artistic prints. They are easy to create and can be sold on platforms like Etsy.

Stock Photos and Videos: Photographers and videographers can sell their work on stock sites like Shutterstock and Adobe Stock. Each download generates passive income.

Music and Audio Files: Musicians and audio engineers can sell their tracks, loops, and sound effects. Platforms like Bandcamp, iTunes, and AudioJungle provide marketplaces for these products.

Membership Sites: Offering exclusive content to subscribers on a membership basis can create a steady income stream. This model works well for niche communities, premium content providers, and ongoing educational resources.

Creating Digital Products

Creating a high-quality digital product involves several steps. Here's how to get started:

Identify Your Niche: Choose a niche that you are knowledgeable about and that has a market demand. Research your audience's needs and preferences to create a product that addresses their pain points.

Plan Your Content: Outline the structure and content of your digital product. For e-books, create a table of contents and chapter summaries. For online courses, draft a syllabus and lesson plans. For software, design a user flow and feature list.

Develop the Product: Use appropriate tools and software to create your digital product. For e-books, consider using tools like Scrivener or Adobe InDesign. For online courses, use video editing software and learning management systems (LMS). For software and apps, leverage coding platforms and development environments.

Ensure Quality: High-quality content is crucial for success. Proofread and edit your e-books, test your software thoroughly, and ensure your videos are well-produced and engaging.

Create Compelling Visuals: Attractive visuals can enhance the appeal of your digital product. Design eye-catching covers for e-books, engaging thumbnails for videos, and user-friendly interfaces for software.

Marketing Digital Products

Effective marketing is key to driving sales of your digital products. Here are some strategies to consider:

Build a Website: Create a professional website to showcase your digital products. Include detailed descriptions, high-quality images, and customer testimonials. Ensure your website is optimised for search engines (SEO) to attract organic traffic.

Leverage Social Media: Use social media platforms to promote your products. Share valuable content related to your niche, engage with your audience, and run targeted ad campaigns to reach potential customers.

Email Marketing: Build an email list of interested prospects and customers. Use email marketing to keep them informed about new products, updates, and promotions. Offer incentives like free samples or discounts to encourage sign-ups.

Collaborate with Influencers: Partner with influencers in your niche to promote your products. Influencers can provide access to a larger audience and add credibility to your offerings.

Use Marketplaces: List your digital products on established marketplaces like Amazon Kindle for e-books, Udemy for courses, and Etsy for printables. These platforms have built-in audiences and marketing tools to boost your sales.

Maximising the Potential of Digital Products

To maximise the potential of your digital products, consider these strategies:

Offer Free Samples: Providing free samples or trial versions can attract more customers. For example, offer a free chapter of your e-book or a trial lesson of your course.

Create Bundles: Bundle related products together at a discounted price. This can increase the perceived value and encourage customers to purchase more.

Upsell and Cross-sell: Encourage customers to buy additional products by suggesting relevant items during the purchase process. For example, recommend an advanced course to someone who bought an introductory one.

Continuously Improve: Collect feedback from customers and use it to improve your products. Regular updates and enhancements can lead to better reviews and repeat customers.

Explore New Formats: Adapt your content to different formats to reach a wider audience. For instance, convert your e-book into an audiobook or create a podcast series from your course material.

Case Study: Successful Digital Product

Consider the case of Sarah, who created an online course on graphic design. She identified a niche market of aspiring designers and planned her content meticulously. By leveraging platforms like Udemy, she reached a global audience. Sarah used social media to promote her course, collaborated with design influencers, and offered a free introductory lesson. Her course received positive reviews, and she reinvested the earnings to create more advanced courses. Today, Sarah's online courses generate significant passive income, allowing her to focus on creating even more valuable content.

Conclusion

Digital products offer a scalable and profitable way to generate passive income. By identifying the right niche, creating high-quality content, and implementing effective marketing strategies, you can build a successful digital product business. In the next chapter, we will explore affiliate marketing, another powerful method for generating passive income. This will provide insights into how to promote other companies' products and earn commissions, leveraging your online presence for financial gain.

AFFILIATE MARKETING

Introduction

Affiliate marketing is a powerful and accessible way to generate passive income by promoting other companies' products or services and earning a commission for each sale made through your referral. This business model requires minimal investment and can be highly profitable if executed correctly. In this chapter, we will delve into the principles of affiliate marketing, how to choose the right products and platforms, and strategies to maximise your earnings.

Understanding Affiliate Marketing

Affiliate marketing involves three key players: the advertiser (merchant), the publisher (affiliate), and the consumer. Here's how it works:

Advertiser: A company that sells products or services and offers an affiliate programme. They provide affiliates with marketing materials and track sales generated through affiliate links.

Publisher: An individual or entity that promotes the advertiser's products or services in exchange for a commission on sales. Publishers use various marketing channels, such as websites, blogs, social media, and email marketing.

Consumer: The end user who purchases the product or service through the affiliate's referral link. The consumer's buying experience remains the same, but the affiliate earns a commission for the referral.

Choosing the Right Niche and Products

Selecting the right niche and products to promote is crucial for success in affiliate marketing. Here are some steps to help you choose wisely:

Identify Your Interests and Expertise: Choose a niche that you are passionate about and knowledgeable in. This will make it easier to create authentic and engaging content.

Research Market Demand: Use tools like Google Trends, keyword planners, and market research reports to gauge demand in your chosen niche. Look for niches with a growing or stable market.

Analyse Competition: Investigate the level of competition in your niche. While high competition can indicate a profitable market, it can also make it harder to stand out. Find a balance where there is demand but not overwhelming competition.

Evaluate Affiliate Programmes: Look for reputable affiliate programmes that offer products or services relevant to your niche. Consider factors such as commission rates, cookie duration (the length of time you'll earn a commission after a consumer clicks your link), and the quality of marketing materials provided.

Popular Affiliate Marketing Platforms

Several platforms facilitate affiliate marketing by connecting publishers with advertisers. Here are some of the most popular ones:

Amazon Associates: One of the largest and most popular affiliate programmes, Amazon Associates allows you to earn commissions by promoting products from Amazon's vast catalogue.

ShareASale: A platform that connects affiliates with a wide range of merchants offering various products and services. It provides detailed reporting and a user-friendly interface.

CJ Affiliate (formerly Commission Junction): A well-established network with a broad selection of advertisers across different niches. It offers robust tracking and reporting tools.

Rakuten Advertising: Another major affiliate network that provides access to a diverse range of products and services, along with strong support and resources for affiliates.

ClickBank: Known for its extensive range of digital products, ClickBank is a favourite among affiliates promoting e-books, online courses, and software.

Building and Growing Your Affiliate Marketing Platform

To succeed in affiliate marketing, you need a platform to promote your chosen products effectively. Here's how to build and grow your affiliate marketing platform:

Create a Website or Blog: Establish an online presence by creating a website or blog. Choose a domain name that reflects your niche and create valuable content that addresses your audience's needs and interests.

Optimise for SEO: Implement search engine optimisation (SEO) strategies to improve your website's visibility on search engines. Use relevant keywords, optimise your site's structure, and create high-quality content to attract organic traffic.

Build an Email List: Collect email addresses from your website visitors and build a mailing list. Use email marketing to keep your audience engaged and promote affiliate products. Offer incentives such as free e-books or exclusive content to encourage sign-ups.

Leverage Social Media: Use social media platforms to promote your content and affiliate products. Engage with your audience, join relevant groups, and participate in discussions to increase your reach.

Content Marketing: Create diverse and valuable content, such as blog posts, reviews, tutorials, and videos, to promote affiliate products. Focus on providing genuine value and addressing your audience's pain points.

Paid Advertising: Consider using paid advertising, such as Google Ads or Facebook Ads, to drive targeted traffic to your affiliate offers. Ensure you track your ROI to avoid overspending.

Maximising Your Affiliate Earnings

To maximise your affiliate earnings, implement the following strategies:

Promote High-Quality Products: Only promote products or services that you genuinely believe in and that offer value to your audience. Your credibility is crucial for long-term success.

Diversify Your Affiliate Partners: Don't rely on a single affiliate programme or product. Diversify your promotions to mitigate risk and increase your earning potential.

Track and Analyse Performance: Use analytics tools to track the performance of your affiliate links and campaigns. Analyse the data to identify what works and what doesn't, and adjust your strategies accordingly.

A/B Testing: Conduct A/B tests on your content, calls-to-action, and marketing strategies to determine what resonates best with your audience. Continuous testing and optimisation can significantly boost your conversion rates.

Provide Bonuses and Incentives: Offer additional bonuses or incentives to your audience for purchasing through your affiliate links. This could be in the form of exclusive content, discounts, or personal support.

Case Study: Successful Affiliate Marketer

Consider the case of Alex, who started a blog focused on fitness and wellness. By consistently creating high-quality content and promoting products he genuinely used and believed in, Alex built a loyal audience. He joined affiliate programmes for fitness equipment, supplements, and online courses. By leveraging SEO, email marketing, and social media, Alex drove significant traffic to his blog. Through careful tracking and optimisation, he identified the most profitable products and strategies. Today, Alex's affiliate marketing efforts generate substantial passive income, allowing him to focus on expanding his content and exploring new opportunities.

Conclusion

Affiliate marketing is a versatile and scalable way to generate passive income. By choosing the right niche and products, building a robust online presence, and implementing effective marketing strategies, you can create a profitable affiliate marketing business.

In the next chapter, we will explore peer-to-peer lending, another innovative method for generating passive income. This will provide insights into how to lend money directly to individuals or businesses and earn attractive returns on your investments.

PEER-TO-PEER LENDING

Introduction

Peer-to-peer (P2P) lending is an innovative method of generating passive income by lending money directly to individuals or businesses through online platforms. These platforms connect lenders with borrowers, bypassing traditional financial institutions, and allowing both parties to benefit from lower costs and higher returns. This chapter will explore the fundamentals of P2P lending, how to get started, and strategies for managing risks and maximising returns.

Understanding Peer-to-Peer Lending

P2P lending platforms facilitate loans between lenders and borrowers. Here's how it works:

Borrowers: Individuals or businesses seeking loans apply through a P2P platform. They provide personal or financial information, which the platform uses to assess their creditworthiness.

Lenders: Investors (lenders) choose to fund loans based on the borrower's profile, loan purpose, and interest rate. Lenders can fund a portion of a loan or the entire amount.

Platform: The P2P platform acts as an intermediary, handling loan application processing, credit checks, and payment collections. It charges fees to both borrowers and lenders for its services.

Benefits of Peer-to-Peer Lending

P2P lending offers several advantages for investors:

Higher Returns: P2P lending can offer higher returns compared to traditional savings accounts and fixed-income investments. Lenders earn interest on the loans they fund, which can be significantly higher than bank interest rates.

Diversification: Investing in P2P loans allows you to diversify your investment portfolio across various borrowers and loan types, reducing risk.

Transparency: P2P platforms provide detailed information about borrowers and loans, allowing lenders to make informed decisions.

Accessibility: P2P lending platforms are easy to use and accessible to individual investors, often with low minimum investment requirements.

Getting Started with Peer-to-Peer Lending

To get started with P2P lending, follow these steps:

Choose a Platform: Select a reputable P2P lending platform. Some popular platforms include Funding Circle, Zopa, Ratesetter, and LendingClub. Compare their features, fees, borrower criteria, and historical returns.

Sign Up and Verify: Create an account on the chosen platform and complete the verification process. This usually involves providing identification and financial information.

Deposit Funds: Transfer the amount you wish to invest into your P2P lending account. Start with a modest amount to familiarise yourself with the process.

Research Loans: Browse available loans on the platform. Each loan listing will include information about the borrower, loan purpose, interest rate, loan term, and risk grade.

Diversify Investments: Spread your investment across multiple loans to mitigate risk. By diversifying, you reduce the impact of any single loan defaulting on your overall portfolio.

Invest: Choose loans that meet your risk tolerance and investment criteria. Allocate funds to these loans and monitor their performance.

Managing Risks in Peer-to-Peer Lending

While P2P lending can offer attractive returns, it also comes with risks. Here are some strategies to manage and mitigate these risks:

Credit Risk: The risk of borrower default is inherent in P2P lending. Minimise this risk by investing in loans with higher credit ratings and diversifying across multiple borrowers and loan types.

Platform Risk: The stability and reliability of the P2P platform itself can be a risk. Choose established platforms with a strong track record and positive reviews.

Economic Risk: Economic downturns can affect borrowers' ability to repay loans. Consider the broader economic context and adjust your investment strategy accordingly.

Liquidity Risk: P2P loans are generally less liquid than other investments. Be prepared to hold loans until maturity, although some platforms offer secondary markets for selling loans before term end.

Due Diligence: Perform due diligence on borrowers and loans. Use the platform's information, but also consider external credit checks and borrower history when available.

Maximising Returns in Peer-to-Peer Lending

To maximise your returns from P2P lending, consider these strategies:

Reinvest Earnings: Reinvest interest payments and principal repayments into new loans to compound your returns over time.

Select Higher-Yield Loans: While higher-yield loans come with higher risk, carefully selecting and diversifying across these loans can boost overall returns.

Regular Monitoring: Regularly monitor your loan portfolio and the performance of individual loans. Stay informed about any changes in borrower status or platform policies.

Utilise Automated Investing: Some platforms offer automated investing tools that allocate your funds based on predefined criteria. This can save time and ensure consistent reinvestment.

Stay Updated: Keep up-to-date with trends and changes in the P2P lending industry. Adapt your strategy based on new insights and platform updates.

Case Study: Successful P2P Investor

Consider the case of Emma, who started with a modest investment in P2P lending. She chose a reputable platform, diversified her investments across multiple loans, and reinvested her earnings. By carefully selecting loans with favourable risk-return profiles and staying informed about market conditions, Emma gradually increased her investment. Over time, she achieved a steady stream of passive income, demonstrating the potential of P2P lending as a viable investment strategy.

Conclusion

Peer-to-peer lending provides a unique and accessible way to generate passive income with the potential for high returns. By choosing the right platform, diversifying investments, and managing risks effectively, you can build a successful P2P lending portfolio.

In the next chapter, we will explore royalties from creative work, another exciting avenue for generating passive income. This will provide insights into how to earn income from intellectual property such as books, music, and art.

ROYALTIES FROM CREATIVE WORK

Introduction

Royalties from creative work represent an excellent source of passive income for artists, writers, musicians, and other creators. By earning royalties, you receive ongoing payments for the use or sale of your intellectual property. This chapter will explore various forms of creative work that can generate royalties, how to create and market your work, and strategies for maximising your royalty income.

Understanding Royalties

Royalties are payments made to creators for the ongoing use or sale of their work. These payments are usually a percentage of the revenue generated from the creative work. Here are some common types of royalties:

Publishing Royalties: Earned by authors for books, articles, and other written works. Publishers pay authors a percentage of the sales revenue.

Music Royalties: Musicians earn royalties when their music is sold, streamed, or used in other media (e.g., films, commercials). This includes performance royalties, mechanical royalties, and synchronisation royalties.

Film and Television Royalties: Screenwriters, directors, and producers earn royalties from the distribution and broadcasting of their films and TV shows.

Art Royalties: Visual artists can earn royalties from the sale of prints, licensing of their artwork for merchandise, and use in various media.

Software and App Royalties: Developers earn royalties from the sale and licensing of software and mobile applications.

Creating Marketable Creative Work

To generate royalties, you need to create high-quality, marketable work. Here are some steps to help you create and prepare your work for earning royalties:

Identify Your Niche: Choose a niche that you are passionate about and that has a market demand. Research your target audience to understand their preferences and needs.

Develop Your Skills: Invest time in honing your craft. Whether it's writing, composing music, creating art, or developing software, continuous improvement is key to creating work that stands out.

Create Original Content: Ensure your work is original and unique. Avoid copying existing works, as originality is crucial for earning royalties and protecting your intellectual property.

Produce High-Quality Work: Invest in the necessary tools and resources to produce professional-quality work. This may include high-quality writing software, recording equipment, or art supplies.

Protect Your Work: Register your work with the appropriate authorities to protect your intellectual property rights. This could involve copyright registration, trademarking, or applying for patents.

Marketing Your Creative Work

Effective marketing is essential to maximise the reach and revenue potential of your creative work. Here are some strategies to market your work:

Build an Online Presence: Create a professional website and maintain active profiles on social media platforms relevant to your niche. Use these platforms to showcase your work, engage with your audience, and build a following.

Leverage Online Marketplaces: Use online marketplaces like Amazon (for books), iTunes and Spotify (for music), Etsy (for art), and app stores (for software) to reach a broader audience.

Collaborate with Influencers: Partner with influencers and other creators in your niche to promote your work. Influencers can help you reach a wider audience and add credibility to your work.

SEO and Content Marketing: Optimise your online content for search engines to attract organic traffic. Create valuable and relevant content that addresses your audience's needs and interests.

Email Marketing: Build an email list of subscribers who are interested in your work. Use email marketing to keep them informed about new releases, promotions, and updates.

Maximising Your Royalty Income

To maximise your royalty income, consider these strategies:

Diversify Your Portfolio: Create multiple works across different formats and platforms. For example, an author might write books, articles, and e-books, while a musician could release singles, albums, and soundtracks.

Negotiate Fair Contracts: When signing contracts with publishers, record labels, or licensing companies, ensure you negotiate fair royalty rates and terms. Seek legal advice if necessary to protect your interests.

Monitor Sales and Royalties: Keep track of your sales and royalty statements to understand which works are performing well and why. Use this information to guide your future projects and marketing efforts.

Expand Your Reach: Explore international markets and distribution channels to increase the exposure and sales of your work. Translation, localisation, and partnerships with foreign distributors can help reach a global audience.

Stay Informed: Keep up-to-date with trends and changes in your industry. This will help you adapt to new opportunities and maximise your earning potential.

Case Study: Successful Royalty Earner

Consider the case of Tom, a musician who started by recording and self-releasing his music on platforms like Bandcamp and SoundCloud. As he built a following, he signed with a record label that helped distribute his music on major streaming platforms. By consistently creating high-quality music, engaging with his audience on social media, and exploring licensing opportunities for films and commercials, Tom steadily increased his royalty income. Today, he enjoys a significant passive income from his music royalties, allowing him to focus on new creative projects.

Conclusion

Earning royalties from creative work is a rewarding way to generate passive income. By creating high-quality, marketable work and effectively marketing it, you can build a steady stream of royalty income.

In the next chapter, we will explore investing in the stock market, another powerful method for generating passive income. This will provide insights into building a portfolio of dividend-paying stocks and other investment strategies to create a reliable income stream.

INVESTING IN THE STOCK MARKET

Introduction

Investing in the stock market is a proven method for generating passive income and building long-term wealth. By purchasing shares of companies, investors can benefit from price appreciation and dividend payments. This chapter will explore different types of stock market investments, how to build a diversified portfolio, and strategies for maximising returns while managing risks.

Types of Stock Market Investments

Investors have several options when it comes to stock market investments, each with its own set of benefits and risks:

Individual Stocks: Buying shares of individual companies allows investors to potentially benefit from price appreciation and dividends. This approach requires thorough research and a good understanding of the companies you invest in.

Dividend Stocks: These are shares of companies that regularly pay dividends to their shareholders. Dividend stocks provide a steady income stream, making them an attractive option for passive income seekers.

Index Funds: These funds track a specific market index, such as the FTSE 100 or the S&P 500. They offer broad market exposure, low fees, and diversification, making them a popular choice for long-term investors.

Exchange-Traded Funds (ETFs): Similar to index funds, ETFs hold a diversified portfolio of stocks and are traded on stock exchanges. They offer flexibility, as they can be bought and sold throughout the trading day.

Mutual Funds: These are professionally managed funds that pool money from multiple investors to buy a diversified portfolio of stocks. They offer diversification and professional management but often come with higher fees than index funds and ETFs.

Building a Diversified Portfolio

A well-diversified portfolio reduces risk and enhances the potential for steady returns. Here's how to build one:

Assess Your Risk Tolerance: Determine how much risk you are willing to take. This will depend on your financial goals, investment horizon, and personal comfort level with market fluctuations.

Allocate Assets: Divide your investment capital among different asset classes, such as stocks, bonds, and cash. A common rule of thumb is to subtract your age from 100 to determine the percentage of your portfolio to allocate to stocks, with the remainder in bonds and cash.

Diversify Within Asset Classes: Within your stock allocation, diversify across various sectors, industries, and geographic regions. This reduces the impact of poor performance in any single area.

Rebalance Regularly: Periodically review and adjust your portfolio to maintain your desired asset allocation. This involves selling high performing assets and buying underperforming ones to keep your portfolio balanced.

Strategies for Maximising Returns

To maximise returns from your stock market investments, consider the following strategies:

Invest for the Long Term: The stock market tends to reward long-term investors. Avoid trying to time the market and focus on holding quality investments for several years.

Dividend Reinvestment: Reinvesting dividends can significantly boost your returns over time. Many brokerages offer automatic dividend reinvestment plans (DRIPs) that purchase additional shares using dividend payouts.

Cost-Average Investing: Invest a fixed amount of money at regular intervals, regardless of market conditions. This strategy, known as dollar-cost averaging, reduces the impact of market volatility and can lead to better returns over time.

Research and Due Diligence: Conduct thorough research before investing in individual stocks. Look at a company's financial health, growth prospects, competitive position, and industry trends.

Stay Informed: Keep up-to-date with market news, economic indicators, and company performance reports. This knowledge will help you make informed investment decisions and adjust your strategy as needed.

Managing Risks

While investing in the stock market offers substantial rewards, it also comes with risks. Here are some strategies to manage these risks:

Diversification: Spread your investments across different sectors, industries, and asset classes to reduce risk.

Asset Allocation: Adjust your asset allocation based on your risk tolerance and investment goals. A well-balanced portfolio mitigates the impact of market volatility.

Emergency Fund: Maintain an emergency fund with sufficient cash to cover 3-6 months of living expenses. This ensures you won't need to sell investments during a market downturn to cover unexpected expenses.

Avoid Emotional Investing: Make investment decisions based on logic and research, not emotions. Avoid panic selling during market downturns and resist the temptation to chase high-flying stocks during market booms.

Regular Review: Periodically review your investment portfolio to ensure it aligns with your financial goals and risk tolerance. Make adjustments as needed to stay on track.

Case Study: Successful Long-Term Investor

Consider the case of Alice, who started investing in the stock market in her early twenties. She built a diversified portfolio of individual stocks, index funds, and ETFs. By consistently investing a portion of her income, reinvesting dividends, and staying disciplined during market fluctuations, Alice saw her portfolio grow significantly over the years.

She regularly reviewed and rebalanced her portfolio to maintain her desired asset allocation. Today, Alice enjoys a substantial passive income from her investments, demonstrating the power of long-term investing and disciplined portfolio management.

Conclusion

Investing in the stock market is a powerful way to generate passive income and build long-term wealth. By understanding different types of stock market investments, building a diversified portfolio, and employing strategies to maximise returns and manage risks, you can create a reliable income stream that supports your financial goals.

In the next chapter, we will explore high-yield savings accounts and certificates of deposit (CDs), which offer a safer but lower-return option for generating passive income. This will provide insights into how to integrate these tools into your overall financial strategy.

HIGH-YIELD SAVINGS ACCOUNTS AND CDS

Introduction

While investing in the stock market can provide substantial returns, it also comes with risks. For those seeking safer, more stable options for generating passive income, high-yield savings accounts and certificates of deposit (CDs) offer reliable alternatives.

These financial instruments provide steady, predictable returns with minimal risk, making them ideal for conservative investors or those looking to diversify their income sources.

In this chapter, we will explore the benefits and drawbacks of high-yield savings accounts and CDs, how to choose the right ones, and strategies for integrating them into your overall financial plan.

Understanding High-Yield Savings Accounts

High-yield savings accounts are bank accounts that offer higher interest rates compared to traditional savings accounts. These accounts are typically offered by online banks, which can provide higher rates due to lower overhead costs.

Benefits of High-Yield Savings Accounts
Higher Interest Rates: High-yield savings accounts offer significantly higher interest rates than traditional savings accounts, allowing your money to grow faster.

Liquidity: Unlike CDs, high-yield savings accounts provide easy access to your funds. You can withdraw money without penalty, making them ideal for emergency savings or short-term goals.

Safety: High-yield savings accounts are insured by the Financial Services Compensation Scheme (FSCS) in the UK or the Federal Deposit Insurance Corporation (FDIC) in the US, protecting your deposits up to a certain limit.

Minimal Risk: These accounts offer a safe place to park your money with virtually no risk of losing your principal.

Drawbacks of High-Yield Savings Accounts

Lower Returns: While higher than traditional savings accounts, the returns on high-yield savings accounts are generally lower than those from investments like stocks or real estate.

Inflation Risk: The interest earned may not always keep pace with inflation, potentially reducing your purchasing power over time.

Interest Rate Fluctuations: Interest rates on high-yield savings accounts can change over time, potentially decreasing your earnings.

Understanding Certificates of Deposit (CDs)

Certificates of deposit (CDs) are fixed-term deposits offered by banks and credit unions. In exchange for leaving your money deposited for a specified period, the bank pays a higher interest rate than regular savings accounts.

Benefits of CDs

Fixed Interest Rates: CDs offer fixed interest rates for the term of the deposit, providing predictable returns.

Safety: Like high-yield savings accounts, CDs are insured by the FSCS or FDIC, protecting your deposits up to a certain limit.

Higher Interest Rates: CDs generally offer higher interest rates than regular and high-yield savings accounts, especially for longer-term deposits.

Minimal Risk: CDs are low-risk investments, making them suitable for conservative investors seeking stable returns.

Drawbacks of CDs

Limited Liquidity: Funds in a CD are locked in for the term of the deposit. Withdrawing money early typically incurs penalties, reducing your returns.

Lower Returns Compared to Other Investments: While offering higher returns than savings accounts, CDs generally yield lower returns than riskier investments like stocks or real estate.

Inflation Risk: Similar to savings accounts, the fixed interest rates on CDs may not keep pace with inflation, potentially eroding your purchasing power.

Choosing the Right High-Yield Savings Account or CD

When selecting a high-yield savings account or CD, consider the following factors:

Interest Rates: Compare interest rates from various banks to find the highest rates available. Remember to consider both promotional and regular rates.

Fees: Look for accounts with no monthly fees or minimum balance requirements. Fees can eat into your returns, so it's essential to minimise them.

Term Length: For CDs, choose a term length that aligns with your financial goals. Longer terms generally offer higher rates but require a longer commitment.

Early Withdrawal Penalties: For CDs, understand the penalties for early withdrawal. Choose a CD with penalties you can manage if you need access to your funds sooner than expected.

Reputation and Stability: Select a reputable and stable bank or credit union. Ensure your deposits are insured by the FSCS or FDIC.

Strategies for Maximising Returns

To maximise your returns from high-yield savings accounts and CDs, consider these strategies:

Laddering CDs: Create a CD ladder by splitting your investment into multiple CDs with varying maturities. This strategy provides regular access to your funds and takes advantage of higher interest rates on longer-term CDs.

Regular Deposits: Make regular deposits into your high-yield savings account to take advantage of compound interest. Even small, consistent contributions can significantly increase your earnings over time.

Stay Informed: Monitor interest rate changes and be ready to switch accounts if better rates become available. Some banks offer rate-matching guarantees or loyalty bonuses for existing customers.

Use Both Accounts: Combine high-yield savings accounts and CDs in your financial strategy. Use the high-yield savings account for emergency funds and short-term goals, while allocating funds you can lock away to CDs for higher returns.

Case Study: Conservative Investor

Consider the case of Robert, a conservative investor nearing retirement. He wanted a safe way to grow his savings without taking on significant risk. Robert divided his savings between a high-yield savings account and a series of CDs.

He created a CD ladder with 1-year, 2-year, and 3-year terms, ensuring he had regular access to his funds while benefiting from higher interest rates on longer-term CDs. By regularly contributing to his high-yield savings account and reinvesting the proceeds from maturing CDs, Robert steadily grew his savings, providing a stable income for his retirement years.

Conclusion

High-yield savings accounts and certificates of deposit (CDs) offer safe, reliable ways to generate passive income with minimal risk. By understanding their benefits and drawbacks, choosing the right accounts, and employing effective strategies, you can maximise your returns and integrate these tools into your overall financial plan.

In the next chapter, we will explore building a portfolio of passive income streams, focusing on diversification and balancing risk and reward to achieve financial stability and growth.

BUILDING A PORTFOLIO OF PASSIVE INCOME STREAMS

Introduction

Diversification is a fundamental principle in investing and wealth building. By creating a portfolio of passive income streams, you can achieve financial stability, reduce risk, and enhance your overall returns. This chapter will guide you through the process of building a diversified portfolio of passive income streams, balancing risk and reward, and managing your portfolio effectively.

The Importance of Diversification

Diversification involves spreading your investments across different assets, industries, and income streams to reduce risk. Here's why diversification is crucial:

Risk Mitigation: Diversifying your income streams reduces the impact of poor performance in any single investment. This helps protect your overall financial health.

Stable Cash Flow: A diversified portfolio provides multiple sources of income, ensuring a more stable and predictable cash flow.

Growth Opportunities: Different income streams have varying growth potentials. Diversification allows you to tap into high-growth opportunities while maintaining a stable base.

Inflation Hedge: By including assets that appreciate with inflation, such as real estate and stocks, you can protect your purchasing power over time.

Types of Passive Income Streams

There are numerous ways to generate passive income. Here are some of the most popular types:

Real Estate Investments: Rental properties, Real Estate Investment Trusts (REITs), and real estate crowdfunding platforms offer steady rental income and potential property appreciation.

Dividend Stocks: Investing in dividend-paying stocks provides regular income from company profits. Reinvesting dividends can compound returns over time.

Online Businesses: E-commerce stores, dropshipping, and digital products like e-books and online courses can generate significant passive income with minimal ongoing effort.

Peer-to-Peer Lending: Lending money to individuals or businesses through P2P platforms can offer attractive returns, though it comes with credit risk.

Royalties from Creative Work: Earning royalties from books, music, art, and software allows you to receive ongoing payments for your intellectual property.

High-Yield Savings Accounts and CDs: These offer low-risk, stable returns and can be used for short-term savings and emergency funds.

Steps to Building a Diversified Portfolio

Follow these steps to build a diversified portfolio of passive income streams:

Assess Your Financial Goals: Determine your financial goals, risk tolerance, and investment horizon. This will guide your decisions on asset allocation and income stream selection.

Evaluate Current Income Streams: Review your existing sources of income and identify gaps or areas for diversification. Consider the stability, growth potential, and risk of each income stream.

Allocate Your Resources: Decide how to allocate your capital among different passive income streams. Aim for a mix of high-risk, high-reward investments and low-risk, stable income sources.

Research and Select Investments: Conduct thorough research to identify high-quality investments within each income stream category. Look for reliable, reputable platforms and assets with strong performance histories.

Implement and Monitor: Start investing in your chosen income streams and regularly monitor their performance. Adjust your portfolio as needed to maintain balance and achieve your financial goals.

Balancing Risk and Reward

Balancing risk and reward is crucial for a successful passive income portfolio. Here are some strategies to achieve this balance.

Risk Assessment: Assess the risk associated with each income stream. Consider factors such as market volatility, credit risk, and economic conditions.

Diversification: Spread your investments across various asset classes, industries, and geographic regions to reduce risk.

Regular Rebalancing: Periodically review and rebalance your portfolio to maintain your desired asset allocation. This ensures you're not overly exposed to any single investment.

Emergency Fund: Maintain an emergency fund to cover unexpected expenses and protect your investments from being liquidated during market downturns.

Professional Advice: Consider consulting a financial advisor to help balance risk and reward in your portfolio. They can provide personalised advice based on your financial situation and goals.

Case Study: Diversified Passive Income Portfolio

Consider the case of Lisa, who wanted to build a diversified portfolio of passive income streams to achieve financial independence. She started by investing in rental properties, providing a steady source of rental income.

To complement this, Lisa purchased dividend-paying stocks and reinvested the dividends to compound her returns. She also created an online store selling digital products, generating additional income with minimal ongoing effort.

To further diversify, Lisa allocated a portion of her savings to peer-to-peer lending platforms, earning attractive returns while managing credit risk through diversification. She also invested in high-yield savings accounts and CDs for short-term savings and stability. By regularly monitoring and rebalancing her portfolio, Lisa maintained a balanced mix of high-growth and stable income streams, ultimately achieving a reliable and diverse passive income portfolio.

Conclusion

Building a portfolio of passive income streams is a powerful strategy for achieving financial stability and growth. By diversifying your investments, balancing risk and reward, and managing your portfolio effectively, you can create a reliable and sustainable income stream that supports your financial goals.

In the next chapter, we will explore automation and outsourcing, providing insights into how to streamline the management of your passive income streams to save time and maximise efficiency.

AUTOMATION AND OUTSOURCING

Introduction

Managing multiple passive income streams can be time-consuming and complex. To maximise efficiency and free up your time for other pursuits, automation and outsourcing are invaluable strategies.

By leveraging technology and delegating tasks to experts, you can streamline the management of your investments and businesses, ensuring they run smoothly with minimal hands-on involvement. This chapter will explore various tools and techniques for automating and outsourcing, and provide practical advice on how to implement these strategies effectively.

The Benefits of Automation and Outsourcing

Time Savings: Automation and outsourcing free up your time, allowing you to focus on higher-level strategy, new investment opportunities, or personal interests.

Consistency: Automated processes and professional management ensure tasks are completed consistently and accurately, reducing the risk of errors.

Scalability: By automating and outsourcing, you can manage a larger number of passive income streams without a proportional increase in workload.

Expertise: Outsourcing tasks to specialists can improve the quality and effectiveness of your operations, leveraging their expertise and experience.

Automation Tools and Techniques

Automation can significantly reduce the manual effort required to manage your passive income streams. Here are some key tools and techniques:

Financial Management: Use software like QuickBooks, Xero, or Mint to automate expense tracking, budgeting, and financial reporting. These tools integrate with your bank accounts and investment platforms to provide real-time financial insights.

Investment Management: Robo-advisors like Betterment, Wealthfront, and Nutmeg automatically manage your investment portfolio based on your risk tolerance and financial goals. They rebalance your portfolio and optimise asset allocation without requiring your active involvement.

Rental Property Management: Property management software such as Buildium, AppFolio, and Cozy can automate rent collection, maintenance requests, and tenant communication. These platforms help streamline property management tasks and improve tenant satisfaction.

E-commerce: Platforms like Shopify, WooCommerce, and BigCommerce offer automation tools for inventory management, order processing, and customer communication. Use email marketing automation tools like Mailchimp or ConvertKit to nurture customer relationships and drive sales.

Content Scheduling: For online businesses and affiliate marketing, use content scheduling tools like Buffer, Hootsuite, and SocialBee to automate social media posts and marketing campaigns. This ensures consistent content delivery and engagement with your audience.

Outsourcing Strategies

Outsourcing allows you to delegate tasks to specialists, improving efficiency and leveraging expertise. Here's how to effectively outsource tasks:

Identify Tasks to Outsource: Determine which tasks are time-consuming, require specialised skills, or are not central to your core business activities. Common tasks to outsource include bookkeeping, customer service, content creation, and property maintenance.

Choose the Right Providers: Select reputable outsourcing providers or freelancers with proven track records. Use platforms like Upwork, Fiverr, and Freelancer to find qualified professionals for various tasks.

Clear Communication: Provide clear instructions and expectations to your outsourcing partners. Establish regular check-ins and performance reviews to ensure tasks are completed to your satisfaction.

Monitor Performance: Use project management tools like Trello, Asana, or Monday.com to track the progress of outsourced tasks. Regularly review the quality of work and make adjustments as needed.

Build Long-Term Relationships: Cultivate strong relationships with reliable outsourcing partners. Consistent collaboration with trusted professionals can lead to better results and a more seamless workflow.

Combining Automation and Outsourcing

Combining automation and outsourcing can further enhance the efficiency of managing your passive income streams. Here are some examples of how to integrate both strategies:

Automated Financial Reports: Use financial management software to automate data collection and reporting. Outsource the analysis and interpretation of these reports to a financial advisor who can provide actionable insights.

Content Creation and Scheduling: Outsource the creation of blog posts, social media content, and marketing materials to freelancers. Use content scheduling tools to automate the publication and distribution of this content.

Property Management: Automate rent collection and maintenance requests using property management software. Outsource on-site property management tasks to a local property manager or management company.

Customer Support: Implement chatbots and automated email responses for initial customer inquiries. Outsource complex or escalated customer support issues to a professional service provider.

Case Study: Automated and Outsourced Online Business
Consider the case of Jack, who runs a successful online store selling custom-designed apparel. To manage his business efficiently, Jack uses Shopify to automate inventory management and order processing. He integrates his store with Printful, a print-on-demand service that handles production and shipping.

Jack outsources graphic design to freelancers on Upwork, ensuring high-quality designs without the need for in-house staff. For marketing, he uses Mailchimp to automate email campaigns and Hootsuite to schedule social media posts.

By combining automation and outsourcing, Jack has significantly reduced the time and effort required to manage his business. This allows him to focus on strategic growth and new product development, ultimately increasing his passive income.

Conclusion

Automation and outsourcing are powerful strategies for streamlining the management of your passive income streams. By leveraging technology and delegating tasks to experts, you can achieve greater efficiency, consistency, and scalability.

Implementing these strategies allows you to focus on higher-level goals and enjoy the benefits of a diversified passive income portfolio.

DROPSHIPPING

Introduction

Dropshipping is an innovative e-commerce model that allows entrepreneurs to sell products without holding inventory. By partnering with suppliers who handle storage, packaging, and shipping, you can focus on marketing and customer service.

This business model offers significant potential for generating passive income with minimal upfront investment. This chapter will explore the fundamentals of dropshipping, how to set up a successful dropshipping business, and strategies for maximising profitability.

Understanding Dropshipping

Dropshipping involves selling products online without keeping them in stock. When a customer places an order, the supplier ships the product directly to the customer. The key players in this model are:

Supplier: The wholesaler or manufacturer who stocks the products and handles fulfillment.

Retailer (You): The entrepreneur who markets and sells the products online.

Customer: The end consumer who purchases the product from your online store.

Benefits of Dropshipping

Low Startup Costs: Since you don't need to purchase inventory upfront, the initial investment is relatively low.

Minimal Overhead: Without the need for warehousing and logistics, your ongoing operational costs are reduced.

Scalability: Dropshipping businesses can scale easily. As your sales grow, your suppliers handle the increased order volume.

Location Independence: You can manage a dropshipping business from anywhere with an internet connection.

Wide Product Selection: You can offer a broad range of products without the risk of unsold inventory.

Setting Up a Dropshipping Business

Choose a Niche: Select a niche that you are passionate about and that has market demand. Research trends, competition, and target audience preferences to identify a profitable niche.

Find Reliable Suppliers: Partner with reputable suppliers who offer quality products and reliable shipping. Platforms like AliExpress, SaleHoo, and Oberlo connect you with suppliers for a variety of products.

Create an Online Store: Use e-commerce platforms like Shopify, WooCommerce, or BigCommerce to set up your online store. These platforms offer user-friendly interfaces and tools to manage your store effectively.

Set Competitive Pricing: Determine your pricing strategy by considering product costs, shipping fees, and competitor prices. Ensure your prices are competitive while maintaining a healthy profit margin.

Implement Payment Solutions: Integrate secure payment gateways like PayPal, Stripe, or Square to process customer payments. Ensure your checkout process is smooth and user-friendly.

Develop a Marketing Plan: Create a comprehensive marketing strategy to drive traffic to your store. Use a mix of SEO, social media marketing, email marketing, and paid advertising to reach your target audience.

Managing and Growing Your Dropshipping Business

Automate Processes: Use automation tools to streamline order processing, inventory management, and customer communication. Tools like Oberlo (for Shopify) can automate the order fulfillment process.

Focus on Customer Service: Provide excellent customer service to build trust and loyalty. Respond promptly to inquiries, address complaints professionally, and seek feedback to improve your offerings.

Monitor Performance: Regularly track key performance indicators (KPIs) such as traffic, conversion rates, average order value, and customer acquisition cost. Use analytics tools to gain insights and make data-driven decisions.

Expand Your Product Range: Introduce new products based on customer feedback and market trends. Continuously updating your product catalog can attract new customers and increase sales.

Build a Strong Brand: Establish a unique brand identity through consistent branding, high-quality visuals, and engaging content. A strong brand can differentiate you from competitors and foster customer loyalty.

Leverage Upselling and Cross-Selling: Increase your average order value by suggesting complementary products or upgrades during the checkout process. Use personalized recommendations to enhance the customer shopping experience.

Case Study: Successful Dropshipping Entrepreneur

Consider the case of Mark, a 30-year-old marketing professional who wanted to create a passive income stream through dropshipping. Here's how he built his successful business:

Niche Selection: Mark chose the niche of eco-friendly products, targeting environmentally conscious consumers. He identified a growing demand for sustainable products and minimal competition in his chosen niche.

Supplier Partnerships: Mark partnered with reliable suppliers on AliExpress who offered quality eco-friendly products. He ensured that his suppliers had positive reviews and reliable shipping times.

Online Store Setup: Using Shopify, Mark created a professional-looking online store with a focus on user experience. He used high-quality images and detailed product descriptions to attract customers.

Marketing Strategy: Mark implemented a multi-channel marketing strategy, including SEO, social media marketing, and Google Ads. He also collaborated with eco-friendly influencers to promote his products.

Automation and Customer Service: To streamline operations, Mark used Oberlo to automate order processing and inventory management. He prioritised excellent customer service, responding quickly to inquiries and resolving issues efficiently.

Continuous Improvement: Mark regularly analyzed his store's performance using Shopify's analytics tools. He expanded his product range based on customer feedback and introduced upselling and cross-selling strategies to boost sales.

Results: Over two years, Mark's dropshipping business grew steadily, generating substantial passive income. His focus on a niche market, reliable suppliers, strong branding, and effective marketing strategies contributed to his success.

Conclusion

Dropshipping offers a viable and scalable way to generate passive income with minimal upfront investment. By choosing the right niche, partnering with reliable suppliers, and leveraging technology to automate processes, you can build a successful dropshipping business.

Focus on providing excellent customer service, continuously improve your offerings, and use data-driven strategies to grow your business. With dedication and the right approach, dropshipping can become a significant source of passive income and contribute to your financial independence.

STAYING ORGANISED

Introduction

As you build a diversified portfolio of passive income streams, staying organised becomes crucial to manage your investments effectively and maximise returns. Keeping track of various income sources, monitoring their performance, and ensuring compliance with financial regulations can be challenging. This chapter provides practical tips and tools to help you stay organised, maintain control, and optimise your financial strategy.

Centralise Your Financial Information

Use Financial Management Software: Tools like QuickBooks, Xero, or Mint can help you centralise and manage all your financial information. These platforms allow you to track income, expenses, investments, and more in one place.

Create a Master Spreadsheet: If you prefer a more hands-on approach, create a detailed spreadsheet that includes all your income streams. Include columns for income source, amount, frequency, expenses, and net income. Regularly update this spreadsheet to maintain accuracy.

Cloud Storage: Store important documents, such as contracts, tax returns, and financial statements, in a secure cloud storage service like Google Drive, Dropbox, or OneDrive. Organise these documents into folders for easy access.

Automate and Schedule

Automate Payments and Transfers: Set up automatic payments for recurring expenses and automatic transfers to savings or investment accounts. This reduces the risk of missing payments and ensures consistent investment contributions.

Schedule Reviews and Updates: Allocate specific times each month to review and update your financial information. Regular reviews help you stay on top of your income streams and make timely adjustments.

Use Calendar Reminders: Set up calendar reminders for important financial dates, such as tax deadlines, dividend payments, or portfolio reviews. Tools like Google Calendar or Microsoft Outlook can help you stay on schedule.

Track Performance and Analyse Data

Performance Dashboards: Use financial management software or create custom dashboards to track the performance of your income streams. Monitor key metrics such as ROI, growth rate, and income consistency.

Regular Reports: Generate regular reports to analyse the performance of your investments. Look for trends, identify underperforming assets, and make data-driven decisions to optimise your portfolio.

Benchmarking: Compare the performance of your income streams against relevant benchmarks. This helps you gauge their effectiveness and make informed adjustments.

Stay Compliant with Regulations

Understand Tax Implications: Keep abreast of the tax implications for each of your income streams. Ensure you understand the requirements for reporting and paying taxes on different types of income.

Hire a Tax Professional: Consider working with a tax advisor to help you navigate complex tax regulations and ensure compliance. A professional can also provide strategies to minimise your tax liability.

Keep Detailed Records: Maintain detailed records of all income, expenses, and transactions. This documentation is essential for accurate tax reporting and can help resolve any disputes or audits.

Leverage Technology and Tools

Investment Tracking Apps: Use apps like Personal Capital, YNAB (You Need a Budget), or Portfolio Performance to track your investments and net worth. These apps provide a comprehensive view of your financial health.

Expense Tracking Tools: Tools like Expensify or Wave can help you track and categorise expenses related to your income streams. This simplifies budgeting and tax preparation.

Project Management Software: For managing tasks and projects related to your income streams, consider using project management tools like Trello, Asana, or Monday.com. These platforms help you organise tasks, set deadlines, and collaborate with team members.

Develop Efficient Systems and Processes

Standardise Procedures: Create standard operating procedures (SOPs) for managing each income stream. Document these procedures to ensure consistency and efficiency.

Delegate and Outsource: Identify tasks that can be delegated or outsourced to free up your time for strategic decision-making. Use freelancers or professional services for tasks like bookkeeping, marketing, or property management.

Continuous Improvement: Regularly review and refine your systems and processes. Seek feedback, identify areas for improvement, and implement changes to enhance efficiency and productivity.

Case Study: Organised Investor

Consider the case of Sarah, an investor with multiple passive income streams, including rental properties, dividend stocks, an online business, and peer-to-peer lending. Here's how she stays organised:

Centralised Management: Sarah uses QuickBooks to centralise all her financial information. She also maintains a detailed spreadsheet for a quick overview of her income streams.

Automation and Scheduling: She sets up automatic payments for expenses and transfers to investment accounts. Sarah schedules monthly reviews to update her financial information and assess performance.

Performance Tracking: Sarah uses Personal Capital to track her investments and generate performance reports. She benchmarks her returns against market indices to evaluate effectiveness.

Compliance and Record-Keeping: Sarah works with a tax advisor to ensure compliance and optimise her tax strategy. She keeps detailed records in cloud storage for easy access and organisation.

Leveraging Technology: She uses Trello to manage tasks related to her online business and rental properties. This helps her stay organised and ensures timely completion of important tasks.

Through these strategies, Sarah maintains control over her diverse income streams, maximises returns, and stays compliant with regulations. Her organised approach allows her to efficiently manage her portfolio and focus on strategic growth.

Conclusion

Staying organised is essential for effectively managing multiple income streams and maximising your financial success. By centralising information, automating tasks, leveraging technology, and developing efficient systems, you can maintain control and optimise your financial strategy. Implement these strategies to stay organised, reduce stress, and ensure the long-term success of your passive income portfolio.

TAX STRATEGIES FOR PASSIVE INCOME

Introduction

Effectively managing taxes is crucial for maximising your net returns from passive income streams. Understanding the tax implications of different investments and utilising tax-efficient strategies can significantly enhance your financial outcomes.

This chapter will explore various tax considerations and strategies to help you minimise your tax liability and retain more of your earnings from passive income.

Understanding Passive Income Taxation

Different types of passive income are subject to various tax rules and rates. Here's an overview of how common passive income streams are taxed:

Dividends: In the UK, dividends have a tax-free allowance, and any dividends above this threshold are taxed at rates depending on your income tax band. In the US, qualified dividends are taxed at lower capital gains rates, while ordinary dividends are taxed as regular income.

Rental Income: Rental income is generally taxed as ordinary income. However, you can deduct expenses related to the property, such as a certain percentage of mortgage interest, maintenance, property management fees, and depreciation, to reduce your taxable income. Please check this, as the rules are changing all the time.

Interest Income: Interest from savings accounts, bonds, and CDs is typically taxed as ordinary income. In the UK, there is a Personal Savings Allowance that allows basic and higher-rate taxpayers to earn a certain amount of interest tax-free.

Capital Gains: Profits from the sale of investments like stocks, real estate, and digital assets are subject to capital gains tax. Long-term capital gains (assets held for more than a year) are usually taxed at lower rates than short-term gains.

Royalties: Royalties earned from creative works or patents are generally taxed as ordinary income. However, expenses related to producing and marketing your work can be deducted.

Tax-Advantaged Accounts

Utilising tax-advantaged accounts can help you defer or reduce taxes on your passive income. Here are some common types of tax-advantaged accounts:

Individual Savings Accounts (ISAs): In the UK, ISAs allow you to earn interest, dividends, and capital gains tax-free. There are different types of ISAs, including Cash ISAs, Stocks and Shares ISAs, and Innovative Finance ISAs, each catering to different investment preferences.

Pension Plans: Contributions to pension plans, such as a Self-Invested Personal Pension (SIPP) in the UK, are tax-deductible, reducing your taxable income. Investment growth within the pension is tax-deferred until withdrawal.

401(k) and IRAs: In the US, contributions to 401(k) plans and Individual Retirement Accounts (IRAs) can be tax-deductible, with investment growth tax-deferred. Roth IRAs offer tax-free withdrawals in retirement.

Health Savings Accounts (HSAs): In the US, HSAs provide triple tax advantages: contributions are tax-deductible, investment growth is tax-deferred, and withdrawals for qualified medical expenses are tax-free.

Tax Deductions and Credits

Taking advantage of tax deductions and credits can further reduce your taxable income. Here are some strategies to consider:

Business Expenses: If you earn passive income from a business or side hustle, deduct legitimate business expenses, such as office supplies, advertising, and travel costs.

Depreciation: For rental properties, depreciate the property over its useful life to reduce your taxable rental income. Depreciation can be a significant tax-saving tool for real estate investors.

Mortgage Interest: Deduct mortgage interest on rental properties to lower your taxable rental income. In some cases, mortgage interest on a personal residence may also be deductible.

Home Office Deduction: If you use part of your home exclusively for business, you may qualify for a home office deduction, allowing you to deduct a portion of your housing expenses.

Tax Credits: Explore available tax credits, such as the Earned Income Tax Credit (EITC) in the US or the Research and Development (R&D) Tax Credit in the UK. Tax credits directly reduce your tax liability and can provide significant savings.

Tax-Efficient Investment Strategies

Implementing tax-efficient investment strategies can help you minimise taxes on your passive income. Here are some approaches to consider:

Asset Location: Place tax-inefficient investments, such as bonds and real estate investment trusts (REITs), in tax-advantaged accounts, while holding tax-efficient investments, like index funds and growth stocks, in taxable accounts.

Tax-Loss Harvesting: Offset capital gains by selling investments at a loss. This strategy can help reduce your overall tax liability and optimise your investment returns.

Dividend Reinvestment Plans (DRIPs): Use DRIPs to automatically reinvest dividends, compounding your returns over time. While dividends are still taxed, the reinvestment can enhance long-term growth.

Long-Term Investing: Hold investments for more than a year to benefit from lower long-term capital gains tax rates. This strategy encourages a long-term perspective and can reduce tax liability.

Gifting and Estate Planning: Consider gifting appreciated assets to family members in lower tax brackets or setting up trusts to manage and distribute wealth tax-efficiently.

Working with Tax Professionals

Navigating the complexities of tax laws and regulations can be challenging. Working with tax professionals, such as accountants or tax advisors, can provide several benefits:

Expertise: Tax professionals stay up-to-date with the latest tax laws and regulations, ensuring you take advantage of all available deductions and credits.

Personalised Advice: A tax advisor can provide personalised strategies based on your unique financial situation and goals, optimising your tax planning efforts.

Audit Support: In the event of an audit, a tax professional can represent you and help resolve any issues with tax authorities.

Peace of Mind: Knowing that your taxes are being managed by an expert can provide peace of mind, allowing you to focus on growing your passive income streams.

Case Study: Tax-Efficient Investor

Consider the case of David, who has built a diverse portfolio of passive income streams, including dividend stocks, rental properties, and an online business. By working with a tax advisor, David implemented several tax-efficient strategies:

Utilised ISAs and SIPPs: David maximised his contributions to ISAs and SIPPs, sheltering a significant portion of his investment income from taxes.

Deducted Rental Property Expenses: He deducted mortgage interest, maintenance costs, and depreciation on his rental properties, reducing his taxable rental income.

Optimised Asset Location: David held tax-efficient investments in taxable accounts and tax-inefficient investments in his ISAs and SIPPs, minimising his overall tax liability.

Engaged in Tax-Loss Harvesting: He regularly reviewed his portfolio to identify opportunities for tax-loss harvesting, offsetting capital gains with losses to lower his tax bill.

Planned for the Long Term: By focusing on long-term investments, David benefited from lower capital gains tax rates, further enhancing his after-tax returns.

Through these strategies, David significantly reduced his tax liability and maximised his net returns, demonstrating the power of effective tax planning for passive income.

Conclusion

Tax-efficient strategies are essential for maximising your net returns from passive income streams. By understanding the tax implications of different investments, utilising tax-advantaged accounts, taking advantage of deductions and credits, and working with tax professionals, you can minimise your tax liability and retain more of your earnings. In the next chapter, we will explore overcoming challenges and staying motivated, providing insights into how to navigate obstacles and maintain your commitment to building a successful passive income portfolio.

OVERCOMING CHALLENGES AND STAYING MOTIVATED

Introduction

Building a portfolio of passive income streams is a long-term endeavour that requires patience, perseverance, and resilience. Along the way, you may encounter various challenges that can test your resolve and commitment.

This chapter will explore common obstacles you might face and provide strategies to overcome them. Additionally, we will discuss ways to stay motivated and maintain your focus on achieving financial independence through passive income.

Common Challenges in Building Passive Income Streams

Initial Capital Requirements: Many passive income streams require an upfront investment, whether in time, money, or both. Accumulating the necessary capital can be challenging, especially if you have other financial obligations.

Time Management: Balancing the demands of building passive income streams with other responsibilities, such as a full-time job, family, and personal commitments, can be difficult.

Market Volatility: Investments such as stocks and real estate can be subject to market fluctuations, which may affect your income and overall financial stability.

Maintaining Quality: Ensuring the consistent quality of your products or services is crucial for sustaining passive income. This can be particularly challenging if you have multiple income streams.

Regulatory Changes: Changes in laws and regulations can impact your income streams, particularly in areas like real estate, taxation, and online businesses.

Technological Advances: Keeping up with technological changes and trends is essential, especially if your income streams rely on digital platforms or online businesses.

Strategies for Overcoming Challenges

Start Small and Scale Up: Begin with a modest investment that you can afford and gradually scale up as you gain experience and accumulate more capital. This approach reduces risk and allows you to learn and adapt without significant financial strain.

Set Realistic Goals: Break down your long-term financial goals into smaller, achievable milestones. Celebrate your progress at each stage to maintain motivation and momentum.

Educate Yourself: Continuously educate yourself about your chosen income streams. Read books, attend seminars, and join online forums to stay informed and improve your skills.

Create a Time Management Plan: Develop a schedule that allocates specific times for working on your passive income streams. Prioritise tasks and eliminate distractions to make the most of your available time.

Diversify Your Income Streams: Spread your investments across different asset classes and industries to reduce risk and mitigate the impact of market volatility.

Seek Professional Advice: Consult financial advisors, tax professionals, and other experts to navigate complex regulations and optimise your financial strategies.

Embrace Technology: Stay updated with the latest technological trends and tools that can enhance your income streams. Invest in automation and outsourcing to streamline operations and maintain quality.

Staying Motivated

Maintaining motivation is crucial for long-term success in building passive income streams. Here are some strategies to help you stay focused and driven:

Visualise Your Goals: Create a vision board or write down your financial goals and place them where you can see them daily. Visual reminders can help keep you focused and motivated.

Track Your Progress: Regularly review your progress towards your goals. Seeing tangible results, such as increased income or investment growth, can boost your motivation and confidence.

Connect with Like-Minded Individuals: Join online communities, attend networking events, and connect with others who share your financial goals. Sharing experiences and learning from others can provide inspiration and support.

Reward Yourself: Celebrate your achievements, no matter how small. Rewarding yourself for reaching milestones can provide positive reinforcement and keep you motivated.

Stay Flexible: Be prepared to adapt your strategies as circumstances change. Flexibility allows you to overcome setbacks and stay on track towards your goals.

Focus on the Long Term: Remind yourself of the long-term benefits of building passive income, such as financial independence, security, and the freedom to pursue your passions. Keeping the bigger picture in mind can help you stay motivated during challenging times.

Case Study: Perseverance in Passive Income

Consider the case of Maria, who faced numerous challenges while building her portfolio of passive income streams. Initially, Maria struggled to find the capital to invest in real estate and stocks. She started small by saving a portion of her salary and reinvesting the dividends from her initial investments.

Maria also faced time management issues, balancing her full-time job with her side businesses. By creating a detailed schedule and prioritising her tasks, she gradually built her passive income streams without compromising her job or personal life.

When market volatility affected her investments, Maria diversified her portfolio, spreading her risk across different asset classes. She sought advice from financial advisors and stayed updated with market trends to make informed decisions.

Through perseverance and dedication, Maria overcame these challenges and successfully built a diversified portfolio of passive income streams. Her journey demonstrates that with the right strategies and mindset, it is possible to overcome obstacles and achieve financial independence.

Conclusion

Building and maintaining a portfolio of passive income streams requires resilience, determination, and strategic planning. By recognising and addressing common challenges, staying motivated, and continuously educating yourself, you can navigate the path to financial independence.

In the next chapter, we will explore real-life case studies of individuals who have successfully built passive income portfolios, highlighting the lessons learned and strategies they employed to achieve their financial goals.

REAL-LIFE CASE STUDIES

Introduction

Learning from the experiences of others can provide valuable insights and inspiration for your own journey towards building passive income streams. This chapter presents real-life case studies of individuals who have successfully created diversified portfolios of passive income. By examining their strategies, challenges, and achievements, you can gain practical knowledge and motivation to apply to your own financial goals.

Case Study 1: John the Real Estate Investor

Background: John, a 45-year-old software engineer, decided to diversify his income streams and build wealth through real estate investments. He started with a modest savings and gradually expanded his portfolio over 15 years.

Strategies:

Start Small: John began by purchasing a small, affordable duplex. He lived in one unit and rented out the other, which helped him manage mortgage payments.

Leverage Equity: As property values increased, John used the equity in his duplex to finance additional rental properties.

Property Management: To save time and ensure professional management, John outsourced property management to a reputable company.

Diversify Locations: John invested in properties across different cities to reduce market-specific risks.

Challenges:

Market Fluctuations: John faced periods of market downturns but mitigated risks through diversification and maintaining cash reserves.

Tenant Issues: He dealt with difficult tenants by implementing thorough screening processes and hiring a property manager.

Results: Over 15 years, John built a portfolio of 10 rental properties, generating substantial passive income. His diversified real estate investments provided financial security and allowed him to retire early.

Case Study 2: Lisa the Dividend Investor

Background: Lisa, a 35-year-old marketing executive, wanted to create a steady income stream for early retirement. She focused on dividend investing to achieve her financial goals.

Strategies:

Dividend Growth Stocks: Lisa invested in companies with a history of increasing dividend payments, ensuring a growing income stream.

Reinvestment: She reinvested dividends through a Dividend Reinvestment Plan (DRIP) to compound her returns.

Diversification: Lisa diversified her portfolio across various sectors, including utilities, consumer goods, and healthcare, to reduce risk.

Tax-Efficient Accounts: She utilised tax-advantaged accounts like ISAs and SIPPs to shelter her investments from taxes.

Challenges:

Market Volatility: Lisa faced fluctuations in stock prices but remained focused on long-term growth and dividend stability.

Balancing Risk: She balanced her portfolio by including a mix of high-yield and growth-oriented dividend stocks.

Results: After a decade of disciplined investing, Lisa's dividend portfolio generated enough passive income to cover her living expenses. She achieved financial independence and pursued her passion for travel and photography.

Case Study 3: Emma the Online Entrepreneur

Background: Emma, a 28-year-old graphic designer, aimed to leverage her skills to create multiple streams of passive income through online businesses.

Strategies:

E-commerce Store: Emma launched an online store selling custom-designed apparel and accessories. She used print-on-demand services to handle production and shipping.

Digital Products: She created and sold digital products, including design templates and online courses on graphic design.

Affiliate Marketing: Emma started a blog focused on design tips and tools, monetising it through affiliate marketing.

Social Media Marketing: She leveraged social media platforms to promote her products and engage with her audience.

Challenges:

Time Management: Balancing multiple income streams was challenging. Emma used automation tools and outsourced tasks to manage her workload efficiently.

Building an Audience: She invested time in building a loyal audience through consistent, high-quality content and effective marketing strategies.

Results: Emma's diversified online businesses generated significant passive income, allowing her to quit her full-time job and focus on growing her ventures. Her success demonstrated the potential of leveraging digital platforms for passive income.

Case Study 4: David the Peer-to-Peer Lender

Background: David, a 40-year-old financial analyst, sought to diversify his investment portfolio by exploring peer-to-peer (P2P) lending.

Strategies:

Platform Selection: David researched and chose reputable P2P lending platforms with a track record of stable returns.

Diversification: He diversified his investments across hundreds of loans to minimise risk.

Risk Assessment: David carefully assessed the creditworthiness of borrowers and chose loans with favourable risk-reward profiles.

Reinvestment: He reinvested interest payments into new loans to compound his returns.

Challenges:

Credit Risk: Managing the risk of borrower defaults was crucial. David mitigated this by diversifying and selecting loans with strong credit ratings.

Economic Downturns: He adjusted his investment strategy based on economic conditions, favouring lower-risk loans during downturns.

Results: Over five years, David's P2P lending portfolio generated a steady stream of passive income with attractive returns. His disciplined approach to risk management and diversification paid off, contributing significantly to his financial independence.

Conclusion

These case studies highlight the diverse paths individuals can take to build successful portfolios of passive income streams. Whether through real estate, dividend investing, online businesses, or P2P lending, each journey involves strategic planning, perseverance, and adaptability. By learning from these real-life examples, you can apply similar strategies and insights to your own passive income endeavours, working towards financial independence and long-term wealth.

In the final chapter, we will summarise the key takeaways from this book and provide a roadmap for implementing the strategies discussed, helping you embark on your journey to building and sustaining passive income streams.

CONCLUSION

Introduction

Throughout this book, we have explored various strategies and methods for generating passive income, from real estate investments and dividend stocks to online businesses and peer-to-peer lending. As we conclude, it's essential to synthesise the key takeaways and provide a clear roadmap to help you embark on your journey to financial independence through passive income.

Key Takeaways

Diversification is Crucial: Building a portfolio of diverse passive income streams reduces risk and enhances financial stability. Spread your investments across different asset classes, industries, and geographic regions.

Start Small and Scale Up: Begin with manageable investments and gradually increase your exposure as you gain experience and confidence. This approach minimises risk and allows for steady growth.

Continuous Learning and Adaptation: Stay informed about market trends, technological advancements, and regulatory changes. Continuous education and adaptability are key to sustaining and growing your passive income streams.

Utilise Automation and Outsourcing: Leveraging technology and delegating tasks to experts can streamline the management of your investments, freeing up time for strategic decision-making and new opportunities.

Tax Efficiency Matters: Implement tax-efficient strategies to maximise your net returns. Utilise tax-advantaged accounts, take advantage of deductions and credits, and seek professional advice when needed.

Long-Term Perspective: Building passive income streams is a marathon, not a sprint. Maintain a long-term perspective, stay patient, and remain committed to your financial goals.

Stay Motivated and Resilient: Overcoming challenges and staying motivated are crucial for long-term success. Set realistic goals, celebrate milestones, and connect with like-minded individuals for support and inspiration.

Roadmap to Financial Independence

Assess Your Financial Situation: Begin by evaluating your current financial status. Understand your income, expenses, assets, and liabilities. Set clear financial goals and determine your risk tolerance.

Build an Emergency Fund: Before investing, ensure you have an emergency fund to cover at least 3-6 months of living expenses. This fund provides a safety net and prevents you from liquidating investments during emergencies.

Start with High-Yield Savings Accounts and CDs: Begin your journey with low-risk options like high-yield savings accounts and certificates of deposit (CDs). These provide stable returns and liquidity, serving as a foundation for more ambitious investments.

Explore Real Estate Investments: Consider investing in rental properties, REITs, or real estate crowdfunding platforms. Real estate offers steady income and potential appreciation, contributing to portfolio diversification.

Invest in Dividend Stocks and Index Funds: Build a diversified portfolio of dividend-paying stocks and index funds. Reinvest dividends to compound your returns and benefit from long-term market growth.

Leverage Online Businesses: Create online businesses such as e-commerce stores, digital products, or affiliate marketing sites. These can generate substantial passive income with minimal ongoing effort.

Consider Peer-to-Peer Lending: Allocate a portion of your investments to peer-to-peer lending platforms. Diversify your loans and reinvest interest payments to maximise returns while managing credit risk.

Develop and Sell Digital Products: Use your skills and expertise to create digital products like e-books, online courses, or software. Digital products offer high profit margins and scalability.

Utilise Tax-Advantaged Accounts: Maximise contributions to tax-advantaged accounts such as ISAs, SIPPs, 401(k)s, and IRAs. These accounts offer tax benefits that enhance your overall returns.

Automate and Outsource: Implement automation tools and outsource tasks to manage your investments efficiently. This approach allows you to scale your passive income streams without being overwhelmed by daily tasks.

Regularly Review and Rebalance Your Portfolio: Periodically assess the performance of your investments and adjust your portfolio to maintain your desired asset allocation. Rebalancing helps manage risk and optimise returns.

Seek Professional Advice: Consult financial advisors, tax professionals, and other experts to guide your investment decisions and ensure compliance with regulations. Professional advice can provide valuable insights and enhance your financial strategy.

Final Thoughts

Achieving financial independence through passive income is a rewarding journey that requires dedication, strategic planning, and continuous learning. By diversifying your income streams, leveraging technology, and staying committed to your goals, you can build a sustainable and robust financial future.

Remember, the path to financial independence is unique for each individual. Adapt the strategies and insights from this book to fit your personal circumstances and objectives. Stay resilient, remain patient, and celebrate your progress along the way.

As you embark on this journey, keep the vision of financial freedom in mind. The efforts you invest today will pave the way for a secure, independent, and fulfilling future.

Acknowledgements

We would like to thank all the readers for their interest and commitment to building passive income. Your dedication to achieving financial independence is commendable, and we hope this book has provided valuable guidance and inspiration for your journey.

Resources

For further reading and resources, consider the following:

Books on personal finance and investing

Online forums and communities focused on passive income

Financial news websites and market analysis platforms

Courses and seminars on investment strategies and financial planning

Glossary
Passive Income: Earnings derived from investments or business activities that do not require active involvement.
Diversification: The practice of spreading investments across different assets to reduce risk.
Automation: The use of technology to perform tasks with minimal human intervention.
Outsourcing: Delegating tasks to external professionals or companies to leverage their expertise and reduce workload.
Tax-Advantaged Accounts: Financial accounts that offer tax benefits, such as ISAs, SIPPs, 401(k)s, and IRAs.
Rebalancing: Adjusting the composition of a portfolio to maintain the desired asset allocation.

www.ingramcontent.com/pod-product-compliance
Lightning Source LLC
Chambersburg PA
CBHW031431210526
45464CB00005B/2152